Sky and C
The Fantastic Fort

BZ BRAVE!
★TRACEY

Written by Tracey Badger
Illustrated by Alexandra Brooke

Published by

Be Brave Books & OKANAGAN PUBLISHING HOUSE

Tracey's dedication: To Holly and Jewels, two very brave and caring girls.

Alexandra's dedication: For Ashton, the bravest boy I know.

Text copyright © 2016 Tracey Badger
Illustrations copyright © 2016 Alexandra Brooke

Written by Tracey Badger
Illustrated by Alexandra Brooke
Edited by Martha Kimpton Badger
Formatted by Jadon Ward
Author/Illustrator photo by Tara Morris Photography

Printed in Canada

1st Printing, June 2016

Published in Canada by:

Be Brave Books
550 Guernsey Avenue
Penticton BC
V2A 1C3

Okanagan Publishing House
1024 Lone Pine Crt
Kelowna BC
V1P 1M7

Library and Archives Canada Cataloguing in Publication
Badger, Tracey, author
Sky and Carey: the fantastic fort / Tracey Badger
ISBN 978-0-9948443-0-9 (paperback)
I. Title:
PS8603.A3345S59 2016   jC813'.6   C2016-904136-0

Visit us online at:

www.skyandcarey.com

www.okanaganpublishinghouse.com

SKY

Sky loves the moon and stars; in fact, she hopes to be the first person to land on planet Mars! Her name reminds us to chase our dreams. Sky's motto is: Be brave!

CAREY

Carey wants to be a vet; after all, she already has about 13 pets! Her name reminds us to be kind. She cares about all creatures, large and small. Carey's motto is: Be caring!

It is the first day of summer vacation.

"Ta-dah!" cheers Sky, completing a cartwheel. "Hey, Carey," she calls to her best friend, "My Aunt Joy makes the best pineapple pickle pie!"

"Eeeeww," squeals Carey, looking up from her *Nutty for Nature* book.

Sky and Carey are waiting for Aunt Joy. She is Sky's favourite aunt and has invited Sky and Carey to stay with her for two weeks. The girls have been waiting FOREVER for this day to arrive!

Sky adds, "Her house is in the woods near Lake Glad. It has lots of neat trails around it. You're going to love it, Carey! You know all about the woods from your books, right?"

"Y-es," Carey answers carefully. "Maybe we'll see some cute fawns, but I sure hope we don't run into any rattlesnakes!" Carey is excited *and* nervous because she has never been in the woods before.

"Aunt Joy has a surprise for us. That's why we had to pack a few of our favourite things. Here she comes!" announces Sky.

"What's up, buttercups?" sings Aunt Joy. "I've planned a special project. Listen to the clue: I live close to nature, but that I think you knew. You're going to build something using tools. You're going to love it. It's super cool!"

Maybe I can finally build my own rocket ship, hopes Sky.

I do need a new birdhouse for Chirpy, thinks Carey.

"Hop in, muffins!" exclaims Aunt Joy. The girls climb into Aunt Joy's van and they drive to her house in the woods.

As soon as they arrive, Sky asks excitedly, "What's the surprise, Aunt Joy?"

"Before we begin, we must hike in. Let's have some fun! This trail's the one," points Aunt Joy.

While hiking, Aunt Joy cautions that they are in rattlesnake territory. She tells the girls to stay calm and back away slowly if they see one.

Yikes, thinks Carey. Then remembering a fact from her book she says, "Did you know that rattlesnakes are actually shy creatures? They often hide in cracks and crevices."

When they reach a clearing in the woods, Aunt Joy declares, "You're going to build your very own fort. Will you make it tall or will it be short? This here is the site. Go on; give it all your might!"

Aunt Joy takes out hammers, nails, string, a tape measure, and even saws from her big, bulky backpack.

"Awesome!" gasp the girls.

After gathering branches they find on the ground, Sky and Carey begin measuring, hammering, and sawing. Carey keeps a careful watch for rattlesnakes as they hammer and saw, saw and hammer.

Every evening
they walk back to
Aunt Joy's house.
And every morning
they trek back to
the fort. After a lot
of hard work, the
fort is finished.

Carey dreams up the perfect name:
Fort Fantastic! Sky paints a sign that
says:

WELCOME
TO FORT
FANTASTIC

"Say, 'Cheese!', sweet peas," grins Aunt Joy, snapping a photo of the happy girls in front of their fort.

Then Aunt Joy suggests the girls decorate the inside of the fort with their favourite things.

Sky adds a fishing pole, a scooter, and an ant farm to her side.

Carey places bird seed, bubbles, and her two pet fish, Swish and Wish, on hers.

They borrow Aunt Joy's disco ball and hang it from the highest branch.

Carey draws a unicorn on a huge piece of paper to pin up on her side. Sky paints a rocket ship and hangs it up on hers.

Soon, their things are here, there, and everywhere.

The next day, Sky has a most brave idea. "Let's dig a tunnel to use as a secret escape route."

The girls dig and shovel, shovel and dig.

Carey reminds Sky, "Watch out for rattlesnakes! Did you know that they use abandoned animal dens, like badger holes?"

Yikes, thinks Sky, taking a closer look down the tunnel.

"Hey, Carey, look at this ginormous, fuzzy, green bug!"

"Be careful with it, Sky. Insects are food for many animals, like woodpeckers and frogs. Oh, but it is cute! Let's name it Icky the Insect," giggles Carey.

The last day with Aunt Joy arrives much too soon.

"Tonight will be our final night together," sighs Aunt Joy. "Let's not be sad. Instead, we'll spend the day at Lake Glad!"

While hiking to the lake, Carey has a most caring idea. "Aunt Joy, can we have a sleepover in the fort tonight?" she asks.

"Oh my, we must give that a try," agrees Aunt Joy.

"Yay!" Sky cheers. "Carey, let's race to the lake!"

Towels flying behind them like superhero capes, the girls zoom ahead of Aunt Joy. Suddenly, something goes wrong...

"AAAAAaaaoohhhh!!!"

Sky and Carey scream, spotting a rattlesnake. Its tail is making a loud *chka, chka, chka, chka* sound.

"Quick, this way!" cries Carey, darting into the woods. Sky follows close behind. They run and scream, scream and run.

Huffing and puffing, the girls stop and look around.
    "Oh, no! I think we're lost. Let's stay in one spot for now," Carey suggests, remembering a safety tip from her book.
    They plop down and start munching on the berries they had brought for a snack.

Sky sighs; she wants to be at the lake practicing cannonballs, not sitting on a bumpy log, lost in the woods.

Putting her arm around her best friend's shoulders, Carey says thoughtfully, "I guess we forgot to stay calm and back away slowly when we saw a rattlesnake!" After a moment she asks, "Sky, are you brave enough to climb a tree to look for a way out?"

Taking a deep breath, Sky jumps up and begins to explore the area for the best lookout tree. She has never climbed such tall trees before, but she is determined to help.

To take their minds off being alone in the woods, Carey calls to Sky, "What's your favourite memory of our time with Aunt Joy?"

"Making bows and arrows," she answers, spotting the perfect tree to climb. "Seriously, we practiced all the time to protect our fort, didn't we, Carey?"

"We heard strange sounds sometimes, but we never saw a rattlesnake until today," agrees Carey. "I think it was rattling its tail to warn us to stay away. Let's name it Ratty the Rattlesnake!"

From half-way up the tree, Sky calls down,
"What's *your* favourite memory, Carey?"

"The time we made pink lemonade," smiles Carey, daydreaming about drinking a glass of ice cold, sweet lemonade.

Suddenly, Sky notices berries scattered all over the ground. *There must be a hole in the snack bag*, she realizes. "Carey, let's follow those berries and see if they lead us back to Aunt Joy!"

Heads down, the girls follow the trail of berries. Just as Sky is about to step on a vine with three pointy leaves, Carey warns her, "Watch out, Sky! I think that's poison ivy! If you touch it you might get an itchy rash. But did you know that birds, deer, and even rabbits depend on it for food?"

They both stop and look up. Their plan has worked!

"*There* you are, my little stars!" cries Aunt Joy, who is just up ahead on the path. "Now, let's get to the lake, carrot cakes."

Later that evening, they sit down to eat Aunt Joy's famous pineapple pickle pie.

"Mmmmm, this pie *is* yummy!" agrees Carey after her first bite.

Sky and Carey tell Aunt Joy about getting lost in the woods.

"When you were scared and in doubt, you worked together and figured a way out!" exclaims Aunt Joy after hearing their story.

Sky and Carey beam at each other proudly.

Carey states, "You were right, Sky, I *do* love the woods."

"And seriously, am I ever glad we can run faster than a rattlesnake can slither," adds Sky. Everyone laughs.

"Time for hugs, ladybugs," says Aunt Joy, tucking them in for their sleepover. "I'll sleep right outside the door, just in case I start to snore!"

Sky bursts out laughing and Carey giggles as they both snuggle into their sleeping bags.

Carey asks sleepily, "Aunt Joy, what is your favourite memory of our time together?"

"Hmmm, let me see," thinks Aunt Joy. "Today! Because you proved how brave and caring two best friends can be."

Dear Fantastic Reader:

When I was a little girl, I spent a lot of time outside in my backyard. There were some really huge, overgrown sumac bushes at the edge of my family's property. It was nice and cool when I crawled underneath them. This became my favourite place to spend time; it was my own personal fort. Forts are awesome. I love forts! I filled my fort with all of my favorite things: like my eraser and sticker collections, my super-cool roller skates, and the book that I happened to be reading at the time.

My neighborhood also had neat trails that I walked on every day to get to my best friend's house. Trails are awesome. I love trails! To this day, when I walk on one, I feel like there is an adventure waiting for me around the next corner.

Forts and trails and friends. These are my most cherished childhood memories.

I hope this book about brave and caring best friends discovering the joys of nature inspires you to create and think about some awesome childhood memories of your own!

And remember...

Friends + Forts = Fantastic Fun!

Tracey Badger

Every day was spent outside. There was never a boring day, even as an only child. I was out of the house as soon as humanly possible and was immersed in nature until just before dinner. I would go exploring on my parent's 12 acres of rolling land; gullies, sagebrush, pine trees, cactus and clay banks. From traversing the creek, to climbing trees, to building forts, to collecting nature's gifts, to scaling the clay bank, I grew up with a huge appreciation and love for the outdoors and the freedom and imagination it allowed me to have as a child.

Alexandra Brooke

Forts really are

You use your imagination!

You get exercise!

You learn how to solve problems!

You feel a sense of calm!

fantastic! Here's why :

You use real life math skills!

You explore and discover new things!

You learn how to use tools!

You have fun!

DESCRIBE YOUR FORT

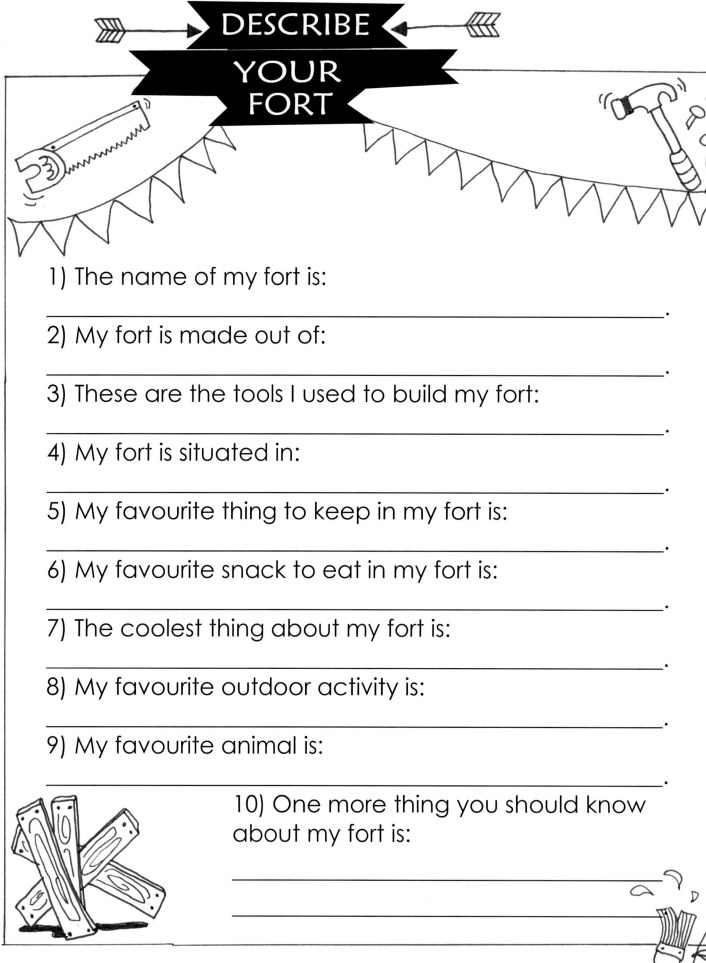

1) The name of my fort is:

_____.

2) My fort is made out of:

_____.

3) These are the tools I used to build my fort:

_____.

4) My fort is situated in:

_____.

5) My favourite thing to keep in my fort is:

_____.

6) My favourite snack to eat in my fort is:

_____.

7) The coolest thing about my fort is:

_____.

8) My favourite outdoor activity is:

_____.

9) My favourite animal is:

_____.

10) One more thing you should know about my fort is:

_____

_____

NAME :_____

MY FANTASTIC FORT

NAME:_____

Discussion Questions:

• How did Sky and Carey find their way out of the woods? Have you read other stories where children find their way out of the woods? How did they succeed?

• In the story, Carey says, "Let's stay in one spot for now…" What are some other things Sky and Carey could have done while they were lost in the woods to stay safe?

• Sky and Carey's names have very special meanings. If you could give yourself any name in the world, what would it be? What special meaning would your name have?

• Sky and Carey both imagine very different things when Aunt Joy tells them they "are going to build something using tools." What did you think they would build? What would you like to build?

• The special items the girls brought with them are displayed inside the fort. Which item(s) do you like best? Which item(s) would you add to the inside of your fort?

• A motto is a phrase that expresses the spirit of a person or place. Sky's motto is: Be brave. Carey's motto is: Be caring. What would your motto be?

• Sky is the brave friend and Carey is the caring one. Can you think of a time in the story when Sky is caring? Or when Carey is brave? In your opinion, is it possible to be both caring and brave?

• Are you able to recognize poison ivy? If not, always check with an adult before touching anything unfamiliar in the wild.

Activity Suggestions:

Build a mini fort: Go on a nature hike and collect items such as grasses, sticks, rocks, leaves, flowers and build a mini fort (use tape, string, glue, and plasticine to hold it all together).

Build a BIG fort: Gather materials such as cardboard boxes, egg cartons, and wrapping paper, as well as scissors, tape, staplers, and markers, and create a life-sized fort (make a village of forts if there are a group of kids doing the activity).

Draw a fort: Imagine the most fantastic fort and draw it (make it big, bright, and beautiful).

Write about your fantastic fort: Include interesting details, such as what it is made of, where it is situated, and so on.

Design a flag: Think about what symbol and colours your flag would have on it, then draw and colour it and add it to your fort.

Decorate a t-shirt: Chose a symbol that represents your name (or the name you would choose for yourself) and draw it on a real or paper t-shirt.

Make a sign: Give your fort a name. Write, paint, or draw your fort's name on a piece of paper, cardboard, or wood.

Find a recipe for homemade lemonade: Make a batch with the help of an adult.

Get dirty with dirt: Use a magnifying glass and sift through dirt or sand to look for insects, rocks, and bones.

Create a summer bucket list: Include your favourite activities, as well as some new activities you would like to try.